Woods and the City

For Atticus Carr
on
Our Thirty-fifth Anniversary

Woods and the City, Peter Weltner © 2021

ISBN: 978-0-578-97604-4

Published by Marrowstone Press,
All rights reserved, © 2021

Woods and the City

Peter Weltner
poems

MARROWSTONE PRESS

Table of Contents

I.

Woods and the City   1
Snowy Plovers   4
Black Rose and Ghost Plant   6
A Muscovy Duck and Mallards   7
Viaticum   10
Three Birds   11
Dan River   12
Hanging Rock   13
Spring Storm   14
Tide Pool   15
Poverty   16
The Lost Boy   17

II.

Prelude and Epilogue   21
Numerology   22
Memento   23
Snowmen   24
An Archaeology of Desire   25
On Being Blue   26
At Jay's Place   27
Marriage   28

III.

A Young Man in Manhattan   33
First Love   36
Hudson River Elegy   37
Vernal Equinox   39
Central Park   40
A Rite of Spring   41
A Prayer   42
The Light We See by on Good Friday   43
Lully, Lullay   45
St. Lucy's Day   46
A Winter Night in Manhattan   47

IV.

Sun Song   51
Early Dawn   52
Early Summers   53
The White Light of Mourning   54
Winter Walk   55
A Stone for Steve   56
After the Funeral   57
Flash Flood   58
Brookdale Hospital   59
Consolation   60
Beachcomber   61
Climbing Bear Mountain   62

V.

The Battle of Buna-Gona   65
Coal Country   66
Cain's Curse   67
Can the Past Be Changed?   68
Classicism (1)   69
Classicism (2)   70
An Odyssey   71
Jonathan, Son of Saul   72
Francesca and Paolo   73
Orpheus   74
The Bassarids   76

VI.

D. 960   81
The Mahler Sixth   82
Rothko Chapel   83
Herz und Mund und Tat und Leben   84
In the Eagerness of Boyish Hope, after Wordsworth   87
Canticum Sacrum   88

I

Woods and the City

1.

The trees
at night
near the lake
were a gift,
a church,
a sanctuary to worship

in if worship
by night
in a church
is trees
and the gift
of moonlight on a lake,

a silent lake
made for worship,
the great gift
of it when night
shades trees
grown taller than a church

spire, a woodland church,
near a lake
and trees
for worship
when night
falls like a gift

from twilight, a gift
of the church
that is night
and the quiet of a lake
where worship
happens by its stands of trees,

oak, hickory, loblolly, tulip trees,
each a gift,
each worship-
ful, each a church
by a lake
that makes prayer possible on a night

to worship trees
shaded by night with its gift
of starlight soft as church candles flickering on the glassy lake.

2.

Sunrise. A new day,
eyes
waking to light
reflected off picture
windows, the joy
heard in the early morning quiet

of a city before its quiet
is broken by day,
roused to the joy
that waking eyes
find in the usual things, the picture-
clear radiance of sunlight

streaming in waves on the river, floods of light
spilling off billboards, sidewalks quiet
as a picture-
book photo until, work day
underway, peoples' eyes
as they pass each other glitter with the joy

of a warm spring morning, the joy
of May light
dazzling their eyes,
the quiet
of sleep over as day
returns its people to the familiar picture

of a bustling city (no illusion, no mere picture
really), the joy
they find in the everyday,
the city's light
(incandescent, neon), the unquiet,
boisterous streets, alleys, their eyes

widening in astonishment as eyes
will do when a faded picture
comes alive in the quiet
joy
of early morning light
as it spills, pours into day,

what daydreams can't quite picture
nor night's quiet, their eyes
alight with happiness, peopled by joy.

Snowy Plovers

The windows of the houses on the Richmond Hills
appear to brighten simultaneously, like streetlights,
switched on all at once. Their moon-soft glow spills

over tree tops trembling in the breeze onto the heights
of the buildings below. Like a long, narrow swatch
of silk, orange-red and shiny, the last of sunset

stretches over the horizon, wet, bleeding into the sea.
I stand at water's edge as darkness gathers and watch
the snowy plovers–small, weightless as puff balls, jet

black in the night–scurry back and forth, almost nervously
as waves rush in and retreat leaving behind the tiny
crustaceans and worms they eat, so light on their feet

they seem to be gliding on the frothy film of water
the ocean sheds on the sand. There are hundreds of them,
flock after flock, steadily moving northward, one after

the other, taking flight only if frightened by a barking
dog or a child's clapping or squeal or sudden laughter
at seeing them, surprising them in the night. It is like a hymn,

I think: how, when they fly they rise no higher than a foot
or two above the beach, swirling together, a black whirling
flock of plovers nearly surrounding me like a smoky cloud,

then landing, en masse, a few yards north to feed some more
on the minuscule creatures the tide brings in. How to put
this? I stand alone, in an unknown sorrow, by ocean's edge,

sunset over, the ensuing darkness like someone's crying aloud
into infinity, as a man might hesitate on an upper ledge
of a high-rise enticed by the beauty he sees spread out

so freely before him, the unbearable sweetness of life like the roar
of the sea calling to him, Come. Come to me. I will restore
all you have lost. Everything. No need to delay. No need to doubt.

Leap. Jump in. The sea and its restless waves are waiting patiently
for you, to feed you. Fledge you, like a plover chick, nesting safely
by shells or driftwood or clumps of seaweed, new to life, insatiably hungry.

Black Rose and Ghost Plant

1. Black Rose Aeonium

Black as a starless night
that casts
no light on earth, limbed
by thin

cane-like sticks, their thick-skinned,
waxy leaves
and gashed,
gnarled roots retrieve

what water they can
lap out of droughtdry
sand

or air, the dark beauty
they've wrought
like a creature raised from the depths of the sea.

2. Ghost (or Aurora) Plant

Pale velveteen
green,
jade pink,
fleshy

stems, zinc-
shiny,
rosy-dawn-colored leaves
tossed by the breeze

like feathers on the necks,
beaks,
and crowns of the tiny porcelain swans

they resemble in the ghostly
glow of a sea-
lit morning, their leaves shimmering, soft as birds' down.

A Muscovy Duck and Mallards

1.

Stranded from its flock, a Muscovy duck
has landed in our neighborhood,
having lost its way, dazed, as if struck
from the sky by fate. It might find food

in the lake but raccoons have harassed
or killed birds there lately, its water algae-,
slime-infested. It cannot last
many days here, no longer migratory.

Why did it stray? Someone has posted
a lawn sign imploring passersby
to treat it gently. Bewildered, lost
in a strange country, now unable to fly

with the rest of its flock to Mexico,
it is a beautiful bird with white,
sleekly black feathers, a red so
intense round its beak when in flight

it shines a brilliant scarlet. I tried to find
it again at dawn or some small sign
that it is still alive, a hint that kindness
endures in things, some divine

purpose I need to believe in. But it had gone,
flown off, already on its way
to Mexico, I hope, no more alone,
rejoining its flock. I cannot say,

of course. I'll never know. Nature
seems to make strange mistakes
sometimes, failures there is no cure
for, all the innocent lives it takes.

Or let's say it is a mystery beyond human
comprehension, some providential
will moving according to a grand plan,
and nothing, nothing on earth is ever accidental.

2.

Back home, April meant the rebirth of oak,
sycamore, maple, sprouting new pine,
birdsong, the chirping of crickets.

I had left that place and would not go back.
My life has followed no design,
pursued no pattern. But I miss the sunsets,

the boyhood pleasures that cling
to me still, a kinder spring's
wild flowers on the hills where I lived,

the joys of a creek spilling
over a dam, the mallards' wings'
iris blue as they flew or dived,

their iridescent, velvety
green heads, brown, gray
and black feathers, the white

of their chests. Reeds, ivy,
thick grass grew on the red clay
banks I would lie on, sunlight

warming my body. Through every season,
the mallards would stay
content on the lake, never took flight

further south despite winter's ice. I've set
my eyes on dying. To go
for a walk round a lake, to be free

of dread, of fear that some net
might trap them as they slowly
drift by or dive hungrily

for food, feathers glistening and wet,
beaks shining-each a measure
of what kindness means, the beauty

of earthly things. May none ever let
it be left uncared for, the allure
of the world, the light we see it by,

like an uncertain theology,
or poetry, our lives sure
of nothing, yet grateful and free of regret.

Viaticum

Sparkling like wet pebbles under a mid-morning
sun, tissue-thin low clouds hang lightly
in the sky. It's a lovely day. Wearing waist high
boots, a fisherman wades into the waves, casting
his line for sea bass. Riptides along the shore
leave behind a snake's wavy patterns on the sand.
Here is where the continent runs out of land
and the journey ends, with nothing left to explore
or to learn. On the cement wall of the promenade
between the Great Highway and the beach, a stubby
stone Buddha rests, an incense stick burning
in its lap. A young surfer drowned near here recently.
So still the day, the air fills with its spicy scents. I prayed,
though I didn't know him, like a man who believes in ghosts
or in some greater happiness than ours beyond all visible coasts.

Three Birds

A pelican, a hawk, a raven
rest on a rail in a tight row,
stone rigid, claws hidden
by clumps of seagrass that grow

from mounds of sand piled on
the plague-closed highway:
a trio of birds, as the sun
weakens, staring beyond the bay,

past the last of sunset to the light
of morning,
despite the oncoming night,
as if daring its frightful nothing

to scare them, three birds waiting for day-
break, to fly
to, high
and far away.

Dan River

After a night's hard rain,
the sky's slate gray,
marbled with clouds
the redbrick color
of piedmont clay.
Woodland sounds,
birdsong, squirrels,
locust, the Dan, rising,
crimson from the stain
of mud bleeding
into it. A whirlpool swirls
near a grassy bank, churned
by currents from upriver,
the headlong, rippling water
near the fork where it once turned

east. Thunder grumbles, pine
cones, twigs, petals
from wild flowers
twirl with new leaves
onto the ground. No sign
of lightning yet. A wren calls
across to its mate. Thieves
of the heart, the hours
fast passing, the restless air
throbbing in morning heat
as winds regain their powers
and flashes of white sheet
lightning silhouette–like lives
left incomplete–the pine trees' bare,
stark black trunks by the pool where an osprey dives.

Hanging Rock

The creek I hike to is March chilly,
the rhododendron in bloom, pink
and white, their tight petals' rusty
from a late frost. Oak, pine, hemlock

twigs, winter-shed bark crack under
my feet. Nearly invisible above
the canopy, the sky is paper
thin and white, the pale sun as icy.

A cold exaltation. A mourning dove
coos near me, hidden by foliage.
Why am I here, too early in spring
to wade in the pool's lucent sea-

blue, to bathe in the falls cascading
toward the lake? The laurel smells sage-
sharp and minty, azalea like clove,
giant moss-covered boulders like mold.

The place of our childhood escapes, fleeing
from our families vacationing at the lake,
the hideaway I am much too old
to hike to, yet I do, for my friend's sake.

Spring Storm

An uneasy spring chills the air, thunder
rumbling in past midnight, frightening
when the storm topples trees over
power lines somewhere, deepening
darkness throughout the wakeful city.

Lock the doors. Close the shutters.
The dead wander through rooms knowing
your pity is useless.

      Water
drips, drips, drips off eaves incessantly
as the rain passes westward.

Lost lives come too freely to the old,
like a knock on the door, pounding hard.
Stay away, you beg, recalling what they told
you as a scared young boy.

        Yet there is no one
here who wishes you harm. Why wait out the night alone?

Tide Pool

Rust and sulfur colored layers of foam carpet the shore.
An old boat's hull, sunken in sand, lies broken
by surging tides, the fierce winds that tore
at it, scattering it like driftwood, leaving a clean,
spring smell in the air. The skies remain cloud-cast
all morning. Bottle shards, shards of seashells,
beer cans, sludge-blackened seaweed wait massed
together in long rows or shallow piles for new swells
to drag them back to sea later in the day. A fishing boat,
loosed from its moorings by last night's pounding waves,
drifts idly, safely near the dock as if hoping to be
retrieved and tied back to its posts. In a pool, like a moat
round a pier, pebbles glow in noon's gray light more brightly
than a string of pearls, a star-like shine to them as in caves
amid the blackened water where they live albino fish swim, translucent yet silvery.

Poverty

Seagulls, terns, jaegers wail
on seal rocks. A stray mutt
sniffs a trash bin. Cold as hail,

sleet-white waves run abut
piles where a dazed man
in scraggly clothes awakes,

startled, his pants, shoes soaked.
He's shaking, fingers half-frozen.
To find salvation, if any, takes

many lifetimes. I wonder how he looked
when young. Tall, beautiful,
I'd wager if every day could be

earth's first. Ribs from a sunken hull
poke through wind-dredged sand.
The man wipes a gritty hand

on his torn jacket. A storm stirs the sea
into a witch's brew of higher crests,
deeper troughs. It's night. West's

where he might want to go. Who rests
elsewhere if not in that land
beyond and below the horizon

he's pointing the way to, maybe to show me
he knows more about reality,
what he dreams of, than I'd ever understand?

The Lost Boy

He was raised a city boy. What did he know
of wilderness? How easy it is to get lost,
to hike farther in than he meant to go, so
far in it is almost night, a surprising frost
chilling the air, before he thinks of returning,
retracing his steps. A lonely, early spring
night. Blinding winds. Few stars. Snow
clouds slowly drifting off. A wide stream too
deep to cross. Trees disguised as ogres, a gnome,
thirsty goblins, a slavering wolf, witches obsessed
by his movements, hiding behind bushes to spy
on him. A child's stories, first fears. Why did you not try
to find him, to rescue him when he did not come home,
lost as he was the night the woods embraced him as one of their own?

II

Prelude and Epilogue

1.

A bone-chilling mid-winter twilight. Frail gray
clouds, wispy as smoke, drift
off high and far away. Snow heavy trees sway
and crack, bend to the winds. The river, swift,
flooding in spring, flows
slowly now, completely ice-bound by late January.

River, woods gently lit by moonlight
on fallen snow:
a black and white
world like a flight
of birds stilled by calligraphy,
made timeless by ink brush and pen.
Soon it will be full night. If I go
now, will the dark grow colder, clearer the deeper I walk in?

2.

Elusive silence, the mute, unheard thing
I have tried to hear in the music I
listen to, not what a singer might sing
or an orchestra play but what might lie
silent in the notes, hidden, not sounded
but implied, like a word never said
but spoken anyway, understood, yet still a mystery,
like light seen through the blur, the haze of failing eyes.

My love, my last hope for reality,
you are worth more
than all the world I should be leaving
before you. If I have told our story
poorly in my poems, tell it for
me better, heartfelt, wordlessly. Do not forget me.

Numerology

I number each wave at its final catastrophe
as it crashes and gently
seeps into the sand, flowing far as the tides
allow, then subsides,
drifting no further, no longer propelled
by the forces that drove
it. Wave after wave dies loud as trees being felled,
like an old oak's roaring protestation
at its fate, like the howl of the ocean
we hear nightly in our bedroom. My love,
when I leave, I will still want you, need
you, long to watch you toss your slacks, shoes, jacket
onto the floor. Count the myriad shells cast on shore, freed
from the sea without wanting to be, our days that many since the day we met.

Memento

1.

Old age is a shattered glass mirror. It is senseless
for me to try to gather its scattered
splinters into an image a friend might guess
was us unless, of course, it flattered
us both. I don't mind I can't sleep nights,
obsessed with the fantasy that somewhere
above or below reality an angel writes
our names in a book where they will stay
side by side to be read by a stranger
some day who might wonder who we were
and why our names are inscribed in it together.
See? Showers have fallen this morning in the park. The fir,
spruce, black gum, hawthorn, loblollies glow
in the misty aftermath of the rain that fell years ago
when my face was your face while the bracing storm passed through.

2.

I try to concentrate on the coming darkness
until at last the sky turns black
enough for rest, though my mattress
needs turning. A green panic–
you'd know what I mean if you had felt
it–possesses me. Love (yes) is two hearts
beating together or two bodies that meld
into one. It is strange how it starts
the same way each time. Clothes on, you sneak
your hand across my thigh as we lie
in the dark side by side. Beneath us the fresh snow
is soft as sand and under moonlight bright as the sky
by day, wide as a desert. All I can ever know
about love is what desire shows me. There was a shallow creek
frozen over glistening near us. Cracking trees. A screech owl's shriek.

Snowmen

Late winter snow has been covering his hut for weeks.
The man—scientist, explorer, mad romantic (in
the stories told much later it is left uncertain)—
poorly dressed for the cold, abandons the compound
to wander off alone. What is it that he seeks
from a world that's all white, more frigid than spin-
drift at sea, freezing his face, coating his hair? Explain
it to me. I see him squinting as he eyes the confound-
ing thing again, his appalling, handsome, near-naked lover
clothed in nothing but snow and ice. Everything is white.
He turns around, takes a few steps, beckons him to follow.

How soon both are melted by their love, by the sunlight
blazing on it, transmuted to pure fire, the snow
enflamed into truest passion that they, together, must suffer so.

An Archaeology of Desire

A life like indecipherable runes, glyphs, fragments
of ancient scriptures, marks inscribed
on dried hide, chiseled in stone, laments
of some kind perhaps or a god glorified.
No one can know for sure. Faded images
on papyrus, a past scratched into bone,
on parchment in pots hidden in caves by sea's
rising tides, the sense of it lost after desire is gone.

I sit in a room empty, white as my mind,
as the chill in the air,
as unlined
paper, cold
as a tale told
only in cipher of a fabled love affair.

I recall a glen (it is you I am writing of), its willows bowing
westward, their branches
drooping, entangled,
a shallow brook, breezes blowing
through trees's leaves
as if I'd been led
where they drifted to discover
your face on coins glittering from sunlight piercing the water.

A longing like a manuscript found in an amphora meant
to store wine in found in a cave,
ruined by damage
from years of damp. What rent
you from me save
desire? Its forgotten script. Its mysterious language.

On Being Blue

The steel blue of loss. The royal blue
of sorrow, of my life without you.

The neon blue of grief, the blue of flood
lights scouring our neighborhood.

The della Robbia blue of mercy, the Virgin's
robes, the tears she sheds for our sins.

The blue of heartbreak, blue as Chinese porcelain,
of your birthstone, of not ever seeing you again.

Missing you the icy blue of Nordic rivers,
fed by fjords. Of rafting their risky waters.

The blue of regrets, of the flawed aquamarine
goblet you bought, your faux Ming screen.

The blue of the sea wall where I met you,
the blue of unhealed bruises, old or new,

the true blue of lovers, the lavender
blue of a field of asters, the blue of disaster,

the flecked, turquoise blue of your eyes,
your torn boxer shorts, your fibs and lies,

the wailed jazzy blue of dawn shining
on our rumpled bed, the blue of my grieving,

the blue of desire, the blue of two lovers
recklessly pursuing the joys of a summer's

sky that was the azure blue of Debussy's
aquarelle music or Hiroshige's more turbulent seas

the blue of the sky we last lay under and made love to,
two blue flames burning out to ash the blue night I left you.

At Jay's Place

The morning light tints the poster-like palms, glass
façades, signs along the Pacific Coast Highway
a translucent apple jelly gold. The close-cut grass
of the lawn, damp with dew, shimmers softly. Our day
is just beginning, the bedroom walls bleached
clean as the sheets. There is a fresh bouquet
of roses Jay left us on a chest. The sun has reached
the tops of the eucalyptus, blazing through
the open shutter slats where gnats swarm
over oranges in a bowl on a sill. Like a creature new
to nature, a grossly fat, furry cat lolls in a warm
patch of sunlight while a caterpillar crawls across
a wooly throw rug. Nothing can happen to harm
us this day. No one will come to grief, nor Jay suffer more loss.

Tattered clouds scatter in a powder blue sky. The scent
of scotch broom sweetens the gap between canyons.
In the cottage next door, a radio plays jazz. Jay lent
us his place for a week, gone back, now his operation's
over, to visit family in Philadelphia. A jet's cattail
trails above gulls flying in lines parallel to the horizon.
A squirrel scampers up a pepper tree. Golden poppies
gleam iridescently. A fanning sprinkler sprays each rail
of his backyard redwood fence, one by one. It is easy
to be happy on a day this brilliant. Three ruby throated
hummingbirds feed on honeysuckle. We listen to the sea's
splashing on rocks from our bed. We are sweating, sticky
from celebrating your twenty-sixth birthday, the love we made
as baths of light washed over us in waves: pewter, pearl white, and silvery.

Marriage

1.

Cardinals, orioles, robins, swifts, blackbirds
alight together, like a flock, near the tulips
my father is mulching–my morning, this day, stilled
by thoughts of him in his garden, not the words
I use here but things in themselves. Water drips
off the roof, the gutters are clogged, filled
with leaves. After weeks of rain, the air's warm, the sky
clear. My father is wearing shorts and his silly,
floppy hat as he works, the grass lush, his flowers
flourishing, claret, burgundy red, butter yellow–
seductive colors enticing to bees, hummingbirds. Showers
will return late in the day, the paper reports. Tomorrow
on my birthday I will tell him I love him. Tiny mites
and grubs gnaw at tender petals. A cat-scared blue jay takes flight.

2.

A witch's ball made of cloudy green
crystal hangs from their porch's ceiling.
Shining on it through a wide screen,
a flattened moon with an amber ring
round it looks rusty as the leaves
stricken by the autumn drought. My father
in his favorite chair reads a murder
mystery he enjoys as its story weaves
its plot while my mother embroiders
an image from Life Magazine of a Lascaux
cave painting of spidery men and bison
in beige, gray-blue, and a brown glow-
ing like wet red clay. Both look to be alone,
solitary, lost in thought, silent and content:
and I, lost as always, late to discover what they meant.

3.

Even as my parents grew frail,
they would walk hand in hand
on a meandering dusty trail
past the lake and a dense stand
of pine through oak and hickory
until they reached their tree,
a magic sycamore which they
would touch, then turn around
to walk back home like a devotee
after a rite observed. Or a vow more profound.

4.

Sycamores, oaks, maples, even a few
birches. Pastel green leaves,
the yellow dust of pollen, new
shoots. May elates me, yet grieves
me too, its massing clouds billowing
with more showers to come,
the linen-white lilac, dewey trillium,
crocus in bud burgeoning, glowing
in the kind spring light. Home,
my father's garden, are my ways of dozily dreaming
on all I've left unsaid, the unending
loss beauty has shown me, the gratitude I regret
I have not yet confessed to you, the sun reddening
at the twilight of a love even death must not let us forget.

III

A Young Man in Manhattan

1.

Stuffed camels, wildebeests, herds
of elk, gazelles grazing   A blue whale
dangling from a ceiling. Pre-historic birds.
Thousands of dinosaurs' bones. The pale
light of stars shown on the dome
of the planetarium. An ancient ant
entombed in amber. A bird's plume
imprinted on stone like the fossil of a plant.

A della Robbia madonna in terra cotta.
Dickinson's Ruins at Daphne. Pollock's
Autumn Rhythm. Dali's Christ crucified
on cubes, hanging in air, no rocks,
no desert, no soldiers on Golgotha,
just Gala's rapt kneeling. Bronzino's erotic
Portrait of a Young Man, smug, well-read,
holding his book tightly, haughtily aristocratic.

These wonders he sees in Manhattan exploring
the huge rooms of its two grandest,
most imposing museums, everything,
each object, artifact displayed at its best,
blessed by soft light and high ceilings,
the past saved, preserved as if forever
from time's pettiness and time's terror,
like sarcophagi from the Valley of the Kings.

2.

Back home, it is a swelteringly hot night
as he tries and fails to fall asleep
in the heat. There is a spirit not right
in the air, the sweet scents that keep
him awake, the sound of hard rain
on leaves, pounding the roof of his family's
house. Something he can't explain

like pain with the force of a need that seizes
him madly. It is late. He dresses, sneaks out
a window, shinnies down a vine,
dashes to the lake. He wants to shout
to the world who he is, to be naked
as Gericault's strongman he lusted
after, to be ravished, to be painted
like him, to be that handsome and fine,
that memorable on canvas long after he's dead.

3.

Sidewalks so slick that one slip led
him to trip onto the street into traffic
rushing past him, lost, engrossed
in the sights. No one helps him up.
A quiet light shines through thick
clouds over the city. Even getting lost
is fun. He tosses an empty cup
of Nedick's coffee into a bin. Rock music
blares from cars. Times Square signs,
Forty Second Street marquees–fantastic,
brash–flash fire engine yellow and red.
A siren whines past him. A bar's curtains
part. A kid his age walks in, his head
held high, more daring than he is, not afraid.

Or to be a part of a matinee crowd waiting
by the opera's lobby to yell brava
to the Met's newest Mimi. A dancer
in a recent Balanchine ballet. Reciting
poems by heart in the Gotham Book Mart.
Or a painter, Rothko, showing at the Betty
Parsons or the Sidney Janis gallery.
A sculptor in the Village. To be like Lenya
singing Seven Deadly Sins at the City Center,
a vast, lost, war-fraught world in her

raspy voice, piano, drums, a banjo sourly
strumming behind her while she repeatedly
taps her foot as the audience applauds more
wildly, louder as their joy roars through the theater.

4.

Old now, he walks his dog by the beach,
the past he is searching for, the long lost
days of his youth in New York not out of reach
of remembering quite yet. But how like a ghost
he senses he already is, roaming a city
that feels as spectral, Manhattan in the fifties.
The sea is calm today, the waves shiny
as the set in Mr. B.'s austere Swan Lake, in places

the water black as lacquer or the corps'
featherless tutus. Why do aged fantasies
stay near him while the new, like offshore
boats mornings after a storm, he sees,
at best, only faintly, far away? Jennie's black
freighter is departing port for one more
journey. Book passage and don't look back.
The Threepenny Opera. How easily, these days, he grieves.

And yet he does look back, back and back
to Manhattan as it was then, his new, free
place, a paradise between two rivers
that is fading now, slowly flowing till it vanishes
like a ship eastbound from the Battery. He
is the paintings he saw there, the music he racks
his brain to hear as once he had heard it, the writers
he first read in its bookstores. His sacred city, holy of holies.

First Love

Summer arrives through half-drawn shutters
bright as noon and glaring white while a host
of birds sings in praise
of the longest day, the splendor of a morning almost
blinding in the air. What I remember
best of that moment of waking
up beside you when I was fourteen: silvery dust swirling
over our heads like minuscule dancers,
a bluejay rapping on the window to rouse us, the scent of rose sprays.

And you and I hiking all day in the forest
after breakfast, the silvery green lichen
on trees, the soft blankets of moss,
shiny as green velvet, warming stones. The greenest
light I had ever seen, the grassy meadow drawing us in
deep into summer with the green of first love, the green of its loss.

Hudson River Elegy

1.

Tugboats flash their lights
as the first stars
gleam like scattered pearls
or earrings a girl
might wear against straight, dark hair.

They flicker, blinking,
shining white,
the eyes
of a city gazing toward
the Atlantic,

watching the sky as
night descends,
its millions of slowly lit
windows in their clarity
staring in wonder at all the river knows.

2.

All that ends in uncertainty, though
they understand they are not
innocent, nor free
to spend their nights
eluding the judgment of what

the river is contemplating, the docks
a few, tired and afraid,
still stand on
despite their disguises, their lies
easily exposed by the Hudson at twilight,

as the moon pleads to the boats
delayed at harbor, "Don't go,"
its light sieved by waves
slapping the piers as each waits
for the sign that it's long past time to leave.

3.

Tugboat lights blink on the river
like stars on a misty,
cloudless night. Trucks, vans, cars
rushing by on the West Side Highway
dazzling it as they hurtle past,

relentless, gazing on it
to accuse it
or to weep for it as stars
do, grieving for it
as in the old story

of a primeval river that, like dead souls'
faces, haunts the hours more
with its relentless flowing
toward the ocean than does
the Hudson whose fate men accept as their own.

4.

It's October. Childhood.
The leaves'
ripened colors, the scent
of apples
in a dockside market.

A wintry wind
slams door after door,
shattering sunset
as the moon slips into
the river as into a lover's arms,

the Hudson headed toward unknown,
foreign ports,
like ships to whatever
destination's been written in
their logbooks where their cargo and crew must go.

Vernal Equinox

The sea's is the way of memory.
Since it is the first day of spring,
I should ask it what "to be"
means, if anything.
Waves rage at the stir of warmer
currents. I climb
up a dune, shivering. A change in weather
speaks to the passage of time
and its perplexities. A man lies
wrapped in a blanket in a lair
he has dug for himself between
seagrass and sand. What dies
too late is the love of life. Dare
to seek anonymity, nothing the same
this day forth. I shout to the air,
loud as I can, "Paul." What does it mean
when I hear in the sea as it rises
toward me the echoing roar of my first lover's name?

Central Park

Free for the afternoon, he strolls
aimlessly from Herald Square
to Central Park, delights in the dolls
gazing back from windows, breathes in city air

as if it were backwoods he were walking
through, a strong autumn breeze
billowing ladies' dresses, mussing
men's hair, knocking their hats off like leaves

blown off trees. The park is full of people
who've left work early, too, lollygagging,
dawdling, basking in the sun, the simple
fact of wandering as if headed toward something

important though nobody seems to need
to be anywhere soon, ambling, moseying,
roaming like angels in paradise freed
to mingle with those they love. Couples holding

hands. Kids darting past him. An elderly man
whispers to stones secrets he alone
knows. Clouds glide by to no guided plan,
serenely as the toy sailboats drift when blown

willy nilly by the winds. Within thick bushes,
he hears a whistle. Laughter. Another,
shriller still. A giddy, playful child rushes
out of his hiding place when to everyone's wonder,

it all suddenly stops. The people. The kids.
The dogs. The birds flying through
the trees. The clouds. The wind. It all skids
to a complete halt. The way immortality takes you,

maybe, with no warning or reason given you why.
He shudders. What if death meant you to stay
this way, transfixed in the beauty,
the meaningless sweetness of your happiest day?

A Rite of Spring

Rustling like fall leaves, the sea oats whip
in the wind. The ocean's deep water
is metallic gray like the sole cargo ship
sailing west past headlands whose shore
has been blackened by midnight bonfires,
its dunes thick with ice plants
like scraggly rag rugs thrown among wiry
nettles. A cottony fibre, a few dead ants
stick to their stems and leaves. A yellow-
green moss clings to damp sand. The ice
plants' petals look hand-painted, row after row
of pale chalky colors: pink, orange, lavender, puce.
Two driftwood poles and a lone tree-stripped, wind-blown,
sea-twisted, bent down like suppliants-bow to powers unknown.

A Prayer

Make these lines the woods where I hid from time
as a boy. And these the days I read in the news
of friends in obituaries, the stories I'm
unlikely to have heard this far from home, sparse clues

to their lives while I was away. In my fantasies, where
I've spent my days, what's needful as before? In the dark
of a forest, tangled with vines and brush, the air
is wet, drizzling, pine and oak and hickory bark

black as duff, the thick canopy defusing sunlight
to a dusky bronze glow or the shine off some precious gold
thing no one can own. Perhaps my mind is not right,
or maybe it is merely the nostalgia of an old

man that proclaims, Go home, boy. The light too soon fades.
So woods speak. Or stay where you are, go
deeper in, make your futile raids
on joy, on indefinable deeds. There's much left to know.

Dear friends. I offer a prayer. May you have lived
in one clear place, never a stranger to it, never
far from the kindness of dreams, nothing at your end deprived
of its beginnings. And I, always the dreamer,

and therefore doomed to disappointment, I see, call it visionary,
you and me wandering together unguided by sight,
miles remote from our homes, romantically
bound to all we've loved and lost, led by our pasts past twilight.

The Light We See by on Good Friday

1.

We trek straight north past the headlands. The sun
is a flat, glowing disc this early in the morning,
a golden pendant floating, rising over the horizon.
The dense woods ahead of us are vaguely sketched in,

misty still, pale gray after a night's good rain, the trees'
shadows boldly inked, broadly brushed as if by
the laws of an ancient calligraphy that frees
the hand to see how the light it paints with is more than today's.

At the forest's edge, shade from knolls and hills deepens
new grass, ferns, shrubs, leaves to an intenser, darker
green too lustrous for Good Friday, sun-blessed greens,
the colors of the resurrection displayed in churches weeks after Easter.

2.

From the beginning, myriad sacred mysteries are lost to history,
the archetypal, mythic, legendary tales that our memories
struggle to recall, false or verifiable. A man Romans crucify
among millions they'd killed died this day. Why did he seize

imaginations, as a poem might do if disguised as a portent,
a promise of better, brighter lives? Yet Mary grieves
at the foot of the cross this noon. His disciples—despondent,
afraid, hiding—wander through Jerusalem's packed streets and alleys.

The birds are at their songs, or mating. Fishermen drag nets
along the Galilee. It's the usual day, despite the thunder,
the storm breaking too quickly, the fierce lightning that sets
lakes and seas on fire, the dark that falls midday, the strange, unholy weather.

3.

In Caravaggio's tragic painting of the deposition, it is easy
to see why the bleak dark background in a picture
made centuries ago was left black as oblivion, Mary
wailing, the beloved disciple doubled over from loss, his cloak

blazing red as if blood-soaked, stunned Nicodemus staring back
at us, questioning our silence, two more women mourning.
The body is being laid not in a tomb but on a slab of brown-black
stone, thick and inhumanly heavy. Where does the light that shines

in the painting come from? From some unseen, foreign sun
that burns outside the visible? Or does it emanate from flesh
and shroud, mortality illuminating the scene, the light death alone
can flood them with in the midst of life's obscurest, most destitute moment?

4.

Maybe it is merely a fable, his story, like the magic of the light
we feel we almost can hear today as we stroll beachside,
confusing our senses, yet clear as the mist disappearing from sight
while lovely wisps of fog burn off slowly, hours late, over Mount Tamalpais.

It is difficult to remember it is Good Friday when an evening
is this radiant, luminous even during our hike through woods
dripping wet and a little bewitched, its trees' shadows looming,
before us, incisive and black as the runes a chisel carves on stone.

We wait, still by the beach, until dusk arrives, route and way, quietly praying
for the sun's return and then look homeward, gazing at clouds
bleeding as if wounded. A child stands alone on a dune laughing,
clapping while trying to catch, like a butterfly in flight, the last good light of day.

Lully, Lullay

Seaweed tossed on the beach, his nerves
as tangled, stipe and fronds, scattered
on sand, dunes, by waves' savage reserves
of power, flattened, the piers' piles, battered
by tides, creaking in winds, wailing loud
as the manzanita trees that cower along
the highway. Loss of what is allowed
us surges in him like a childhood song
suddenly recalled, the words in his head
clear as its tune. At dawn, the beach resembles
a potter's graveyard, flat, unmarked. His dead
lie elsewhere, apart, in distant cemeteries.
Yet he hears them, in the sunrise, singing to please
him as his mother would do when howling wolves
pursued him in his sleep, to calm him with her lullabies.

St. Lucy's Day

For hours, after a year's drought, a pouring rain
is falling. Turbulent far out as the horizon,
miles off shore, dune-high
waves crash and break. A wan, plain
morning follows dawn, the sun
smothered by clouds, no glare blindingly
shining, just a dusky earth seen under a gray sky.

As they reach the beach, the waves begin to clash,
swirling, dipping, bowing, dancing, led
by headwinds whose scent
mingles salt, sand, shells, seaweed, dead
fish though gusts sweeten the air with the fresh
smell of eucalyptus and pine bark, the light less absent
now but still shining obscurely, dimly seen, shaded, refracted.

It is Saint Lucy's Day, a rite to celebrate new light. I remember,
when I was young, girls dressed in red
sashes, white dresses, wreathes worn in their plaited
hair decorated with wax candles whose flames would flicker
in the church's solemn darkness during their processional
toward the altar, the alms given, the greetings offered after in the hall
where cakes and buns waited for the feast in the midst of brutal weather.

And the lifelong power of its mystery, the ghosts the candles cast
on our church's arched ceiling, majestic high walls,
and night-darkened stained glass windows, their shadows leaping
and jumping, looming, almost trembling as the girls passed
by our pews and gathered round Pastor Fischer, the choir singing
all the while the old Lutheran hymns. What lures me, what calls
me back? Low light and shadows on a gloomy day. The tenebrous glow of morning.

A Winter Night in Manhattan

The winds tonight are Nordic harsh. I'm thinking
of a city from early in my life, years ago.
The sidewalk's slippery, fresh snow crackling
underfoot. An icy moon smolders low
in a glacier white sky, in a numbing exaltation.
I'm roaming the Village. A boy's sleepy
eyes stare at me from across the Square.
All I never dared do, all I've left undone
elude me like a dream I can never see
clearly enough to know how to compare
it to reality. If I now fondle his blond hair
as it flares against my pillow, hear Moffo
singing at the Met, ravishing in her helplessness
as Mélisande, watch a Balanchine dancer practice
at the barre, study a de Kooning at the Sidney Janis Gallery,

or after a Price recital walk home in another fierce
blizzard as I listen to the sibilant sighs snow makes
falling on the city, still all my lingering fears,
my old mistakes, new losses chill me like the flakes
that sweep over Manhattan until it disappears–
streetlights, taxis, tenements, brownstones,
museums, theaters–shrouded by a storm. A tug nears
the harbor, people struggle off, its horns' moans
muffled by howling winds. Radio static seeps
through a transom. I hear dancing. I remember
a party. Too many things I miss my mind keeps
forgetting. I regret my life too late to change it. Water
under the bridge, I'm told. Yet I wish I'd lived mine better.
In the blur of winter's baffling air, nothing ever stays transparent.
A boy in the Village once stared at me, and I failed to know what it meant.

IV

Sun Song

Their bark a dark tarnished green,
feathery leaves silvered by fog,
the park's cypresses look keen
for spring. A man and his dog
stroll round Stow Lake. He winds
his watch, squints skyward,
gazes behind him, finds
nothing near to fear, on guard
for danger lurking everywhere.
So memory stares back at a world
as night turns into day, dreams
into realities, like you last night curled
up beside me, so real it seems
still true. I wanted to kiss you but didn't dare

to. Over green hills, the sun
rises in mist, fills
the sky with a quiet gleam,
not night vanquished, undone,
but a hazy light that thrills
me as if you were no dream
after all, not in the way I mean
it, the pleasure that passed
between us a love scene
from a movie I might have cast
you in, if I could. It's all fantastic,
isn't it? The light we see by. A blue heron
nesting in a tall cypress is lifting its beak
skyward as if just awakening, look!, in praise of the sun.

Early Dawn

It is low tide. The wet sand is the tan color
of ripened hay. Shallow pools ripple along
the shoreline, feathers drift in the water,
dogs bark at crows as a girl's sing-song
voice pierces the fog while she walks by the surf
playing, delighting in the spray, leaping in
and out of gently splashing waves. The birth
of day comes slower this morning, sun still low, moon's twin.

I remember, years ago, walking alone in a blizzard
at dawn, barely able to see for the white-
out. Yet, reaching your house, I saw your face
in a window as you gazed beyond the snow, toward
what I could not know. I suppose it was not right
of me to stare so in that morning's barely sun-lit, hazy grace.

Early Summers

A sudden break in dark clouds reveals plaits of lavender blue
as the sky clears over a field of ripening sunflowers.
Still a boy, fourteen maybe, I roam with nothing to do
all day but drift in a rowboat and while the hours
away, waiting for you. A few more brief showers
pursue me, the columbine and lupine and larkspur shining
brighter than before once the sun breaks fully through
at last, petals glowing an azure more varied than the sky's.
A dream as lovely as mine should endure a lifetime
wouldn't you agree?, if reality's
to be measured against everything
it would judge us by especially if none of it is true.
To make the past up, to survive it, ought not be a crime,
should it? This late I see, as if it had happened, my love for you
consummated in a field of sunflowers opening under a sky as fine
a sapphire as your eyes' gem-flecked irises. Why shouldn't I romanticize
boyhood longings now denied me? Desire made me who I am, then unmade me,
no summers remaining to dream of, no nights of us together, lusty and carefree.

The White Light of Mourning

The world is a wonder of ordinariness. Every day,
he is surprised by its survival. There are no miracles.
Just light and sea and sky, the gentle spray
of waves in his face, the morning sun on the sails

of a boat a pink-orange translucent as the roses
in his backyard. After death, what beneficence
endures? At home, he arranges lavender asters
into crystal bowls. What reticence, greater than silence,

partakes of the grief he feels as the last spring flowers
drift onto his lawn, scattering petals that after rain blaze
as if with life renewed, dew-wet, sparkling long past dawn?
They look as if they were burning with a minute bright

flame that is consuming their colors into one song of praise,
startling his eyes with the white light, the fierce blank light
of mourning—like the flare, the stunning incandescence
of the sky, after a storm, when the sun is new born to our sorrows.

Winter Walk

Bored, he walks along a rocky
shoreline, past piers and a long
abandoned harbor, nothing to see
that intrigues him. It is not wrong
in times like these to give into ennui,
when no ships from infested
cities dock in plague-ridden
places. It is not wrong to be sad.
 It is not a mortal sin
to despair, hearts hard as stone.
Gulls fly in flocks toward
the headlands, their chalk cliffs bone-
pale. He picks up a a shard
of a rock with the face of a demon
etched on it that seems to be gazing seaward,

whether in admonition or foreboding who
could trace now. The ocean along the coast
is icy, the white water whiter than snow.
What would it show you if he could tell you
what he feels inside him? I suppose lost,
he might say. It is hard for me to know,
staring down at him from the seawall
though I would guess, maybe, he'd prefer
to walk among deities this morning, the call
of ancient places summoning him back.
Northern lights seen from a long boat. The fir
forests Vikings ravaged. Greece in the age
of Achilles. Or Alcibiades preparing to attack
Syracuse. That is what he seems to be seeking, the rage
for glory. Tragedy. The sudden leap into the sea with no tomorrow.

A Stone for Steve

Speak to that rock before their eyes and it will pour out its water.
                                        Numbers 20:8

A wave-washed, wind-polished stone,
oblong, hefty in the hand, heavy
as a rock twice its size, of unknown
origin, heaven sent perhaps, tiny
bits of crystal sand glittering in it,
sparkling like black ice, a stone beautifully
rendered, befitting a temple, split
off from a boulder to fall into the sea,
tossed by the tide on the beach. A red splash,
like a fragment of a loosely brushed in
calligraphic letter, livid as a bruise or rash,
gashes a surface like a wound. Find a garden
for it where its soul might flow freely, a glen,
woods, a poem. Let it be a holy place. Speak to it often.

After the Funeral

His son finds a few old photos behind a file cabinet. A soldier
slumps dead amid rubble after the battle for Saint-Lô.
Ashen, her shawl torn, a mother clasps her daughter,
her child's arms limp and bloody, as she begs. A broken radio
lies in a doorway. Why had he not told him? One night is all it took
to bomb the entire city out of existence. My memory
of those days, his father once said to his boy, is a book
I wouldn't let you read until I'm laid to rest in a cemetery
where there's no one left to hate or to love. His father
never once cried. Just stared or looked away. His eyes haunt
his son still, years later. A city reduced to dust, wasted,
rent by war. In a gray, faded picture, his father sits by the gate
of a prison, holding a rifle. In another, he wanders down tracks, gaunt
and tired. Would he have loved him better, if it had ever ended?
Or is history made by those who can't forget all that others learn too late?

Flash Flood

The wrongs we do are never through with us,
unmitigated by our hard work
We live in a place wrecked by the constant quirk
of bad weather, no release
from the heat a storm
might cool, the dust it might settle. It does not cease,
the harm
the rain does, the high water
washing away what's left
after months of drought, both a disaster.
Yet you see how we've kept
displayed, to charm its malign powers,
the bones we found in the arroyos
though no one knows whose
they are confused among the skeletons
of wood rats
rattlers
coyotes
gila monsters.

Brookdale Hospital

I notice in photos their frightened faces but cannot
see how each nears the end, or the wheeling
in and out of gurneys, the toll
higher each day, I, blind
from rage and fear, their lot
like mine some day, the dying
confined out of sight, alone: those chance stole
from life, unknowing all they'd be leaving behind.

They are good. They who bring food.
Who nurse. Comfort. Who care for
the ill. Mourn the lost. Oh, magnitude
of death. Why do you stand
like them, your betters, watchful at the door,
vigilant, yet unable to offer a kind word, a thoughtful, loving hand?

Consolation

Rustling wisteria trellises
in late August.
Red worms
thrashing in soggy clay.
A wet horned beetle
sticky with dust.
A boy trapped inside
on a rainy day
gazes out a window
as his grandpa rocks
in a chair, lost in thoughts
of the war
his son died in.
His socks
stink worse
than the dog
on the floor
by the fireplace.
The boy's mother tears
a sheet of white paper,
folds it into a bird
that magically flies off
and disappears.
There's no need to be sad, she says,
using a word
she's refused to hear him say
the many years
she's tried to console him.
Jay, robin, cardinal, sparrow.
All's well.
What flies away comes back tomorrow.
Look, she says.
And it's true.
With two flicks
of her hand,
the bird returns
in his favorite of her tricks.

Beachcomber

An ocean is a good place to grieve by. It sings
at its shoreline of mutabilities, time, the illusory
nature of things, shifting dunes, what high tide brings
in, broken sand dollars, jars, crab claws, the body

of a muskrat swept out in a storm, multi-colored,
lustrous shells intact or cracked apart, no pattern
to any of it, of course, ragged driftwood, tangled
seaweed, nothing worth saving, to keep or to learn

from, not his to question why its waste has outlasted
the friends he's lost. Why shouldn't he hunger
for a better place somewhere? He can remember
how, as a child, he'd use the lens of his magnifying

glass and the sun's rays focused on dry decaying
leaves to start fires so he could watch the wind blow
ashes into the sky, or wherever it is things set on fire go,
freed from time, debris, the residues of some new sorrow.

It's almost night by the Pacific, shade turned to shadow
at the end of sunset, when he sees Bill borne
back to him as if swept in by waves. This is what to mourn
must mean, his memory the sea's, casting on shore its own misfortunes.

Climbing Bear Mountain

This high in the far north backcountry mountains,
the water is clear, good to drink, the air
scented by the black oak, pine, ash the rain's
just washed, the elderberry, spruce, willow, and fir

nearer the river spiced with the sweet decay
of last fall's leaves burning golden brown
under a noon sun that's found a way to stay
steady, timeless, like the sun's eye as it gazed down

on Joshua demanding it remain motionless over Gibeon
until he'd conquered the foes he was sent to fight.
The birds rest in shade rock-still, mute as stone.
The man kneels, drinks from cupped hands in a rite

of atonement he's trying to learn. No earthly creature
rustles in the brush, no breezes waft through fern
or thicket or sedge. What he meant to have done
he did not do. The sun's eye glares, blazing and pure,

fixed upon him. He knows nothing of gods. The mountain
ridges steam. The heat like a green fire burns the earth
clean. A redwing blackbird flies free of its roost. Try to explain
the wonder the man feels watching it soar like a spirit, setting forth.

v

The Battle of Buna-Gona

They were ours, the apple groves, plank gates, pine picket
fences, the black bulls grazing in a muddy pasture.
His and my jacket, jeans, face, hair were sopping wet
from rain that had poured all day as we played, the lure
of a warm early fall storm irresistible to kids our age,
the freedom we had to run wild, drenched, drinking
it all in, mouths wide open. The thunder's thrilling rage,
lightning's scary power were ours, too, creeks flooding
over banks, the trees' branches creaking in woods, twisted
by the wind, all of life was ours, we two soldiers crossing ravines,
trekking through jungles, wary of danger in the war our fathers read
to us about, though we were too young, or heartless, to have comprehended
what it meant until, that night, though forbidden to look, we saw a magazine's
first photos of the dead lying half-buried in sand, faceless on the beachhead.

Coal Country

Water, stone keep calling me back
home, elemental things for lack
of which we die, it's said,
to where he, my best friend, naked,
arms spread wide swan dived
into a man-made lake off a ledge,
cracking his head
in two on a flooded boulder,
the last
dare-devil plunge
he would ever take, survived
only by his mother. The past
is never done with. An abandoned gravel
pit. Back woods. Coal ash. I travel
its mapless roads to see
what is left since it is right to speak of Niobe
again, of a woman who never sleeps,
of rock face that weeps.

Cain's Curse

In the wrathful swells of the sea, the fury of the wind
and surging surf, my city is slowly drowning, a raging rain
battering it. What does it mean, that mankind has sinned
from the beginning by the blood shed, by the stain
of a crime committed at the start no flood might wash
away? Yet I believe it. I might be confessing to a murder.
But I was lucky, an angry ten year old kid who'd bash
a boy's head in in a May rain and failed, too weak. His laughter
had enraged me, mocking me for my spit-filled stutter
as I tried to say what I felt but couldn't. I had a crush
on him. He hurt me. So I hurled a wide slate slab straight at him.
He bled and bled through his hood and stumbled home in tears. In the dim
light shed by a sun shrouded by darkening clouds I thought I saw, alone,
God's eye looking down upon me, cursing me for what I had done,
mine the oldest crime as I hid in woods, rained on, nowhere to go, nowhere to run.

Can the Past Be Changed?

1.

Briseis isn't worth it, Achilles says,
takes Patroclus by the hand, sails
to Thessaly to spend their days
tilling fields. Rebelling, Joshua rails

against Jahweh, refuses to obey
his commands, bypasses Jericho
to settle in a desert to pray,
unbloodied, in peace. In his arms, Dido

is charmed by Aeneas. Who will miss
Rome if I never found it, he whispers
in her ears. I choose, my dear, bliss
with you, not destiny with its endless wars.

2.

July 1st. The Somme. Generals
Hague, Joffre, von Gallwitz.
The first barrage. One man falls,
among thousands. His photo sits

on his wife's nightstand, her husband
smiling proudly in his uniform.
What does she see? The land,
desolate where he fought in the storm

of battle and him lying in no cemetery
but a bombed-out crater. It is,
she says years later, my story,
no re-write possible after so many losses.

Classicism (1)

Lovers of ancient rites, lovers
of mythic places, each time
you die may you shine brighter,
each time. Louder and louder,

waves break on the shoreline
as Demosthenes orates over
their roaring. Nothing is easier
than men's self-deceit. We stand

as we had stood, millennia ago,
seaside, hand in hand,
as a lone black swan gleams
in twilight. O Mávros Thánatos.

Nothing is as it first seems.
It is a deathly deity, no
bird, you feel in the loss
of knowledge flashing off its feathers.

Classicism (2)

Laden with massive crates,
two cargo ships rest
by the Golden Gate's
portal. The bay is dark
as pitch or tar. West-
bound, two ships embark
from harbor, hard
to see in the headland's
shadows despite the mast-
heads, the red sidelights.
Penumbral matters. A shard
inscribed with things long past.
Long ships. Or triremes Xenophon writes
of. This sea I stand by. These ancient strands.

An Odyssey

He wants to return home, but it's a long way
back and he has been gone many years.
He is no flâneur, no traveler, has little to say
to people he meets on streets and fears
their curious glances. What if his journey
took him to alien places? To talk
with the dead, for instance. Or sail at sea,
lost in storms. Fight giants that stalk
him in nightmare caves. Spy on a youth
rising naked after bathing in a stream.
A witch who entices him to see the truth
of the beast he has become in his dream-
life. Suppose he enjoys pleasuring a seer
who will grant him immortality provided he will stay
on his island forever, inhabited only by deer
and rabbits and goats and every day facing each other.

Or, what if, once back, he does not want to be there,
does not like what he sees in the least. Another
trip might kill him at his age. Why should he dare
it? Yet perhaps he should go. By car, boat, plane.
Maybe find himself in a distant desert kingdom
where none have seen either oceans or the sea
or know what the word 'voyage' means. Where no rain
ever falls. Whose people thrive by being numb
to loss, survive on desiccation and the secrecy
they feed on. They long to remain as they are, come
what might. Stay always thirsty, hungry. Permit
no joy. There is no better country to rest in than a waste
land, no better place to die in, he believes, weary
of traveling, than among a destitute people one taste
of the past might have poisoned, left them all feeling desperate
to understand a foreigner's tongue. Try it. Say, 'History.' 'Poetry.' 'Home.'

Jonathan, Son of Saul

1.

Sorely famished, he unknowingly disobeyed his father
by dipping his warrior's staff deep into a forest's floor
heavy with honey, eating despite the king's mad order
for his men to take no nourishment by day before
victory was theirs, sipping the sticky honey spread
in aureate pools thick as butter, not slowly dripped
from combs but spilled like wine gone straight to his head
the moment he ate it, all his desire's doubts stripped
from eyes made brighter by what he had devoured. And so
he must die that night, his life destroyed by a father's vow
to slaughter those who fed their hunger, failure to know
no excuse. But his friends, true comrades, would not allow
it, threatening rebellion, imploring, as a lover might have sung
of sooner to him, how sweet it was to taste, how golden on the tongue.

2.

And it came to pass in a time of the nation's desolation
that his father falls from favor, half-mad, losing the power
he had known over his people, his wives, and Jonathan, the son
who failed him like God. And he conjures a Witch of Endor
to rise out of the cave of his terror and hears that he
is done for soon and so demands his son choose, lover
or him, in the internecine wars that will follow surely
as his father's hatred had after he had seen his son's hunger
for dates and figs and wine satisfied as he lay in bed,
naked, sung to by the man who would supplant him, greedy
for more in his ambitious, libidinous ways, this upstart David,
a sweet singer, yes, though a subtler liar. But look, Saul, now. See
how he weeps for you and your boy, laments the love he has lost surpassing
the love of women, wonderful, and you, the fallen, who ruined lives for nothing.

Francesca and Paolo

Adulterous lovers, murdered together, they cannot
not see each other, circling, swirling
in a ceaseless storm, cannot not know
the woe of lost bliss, two forsaken
souls bound in one tight knot,
the painful cincture of a last embrace, twirling
in the whirlwind of what Dante deems lust, the tornado
desire turns into when Love's hard laws are violated or forgotten.

The poet faints at their fate. Why is it right, good,
they are punished bearing the scars
of the stiletto that brought them to hell? Oh, magnitude
of passion. Why can't Dante
see it?, Paolo Malatesta, Francesca da Rimini
doomed for what moved them as it does the sun and other stars.

Orpheus

1.

Well, then, memory is a mirror you can swim
through to the other side where your past
presides like a jury. The light there is dim,
the winds storm-strong. I have to hold fast
to a wall or door or a strange hand to keep
from being blown off my feet. Should I embrace
the tribunal's sentence? How can I sleep
now and risk losing him again, seeing his face
in my dreams since dreams are mirrors, too,
and so dooming him to die twice from my need
to love him more than he can bear? What do
I do? I can hear him weep, I can hear him plead
with me not to look. But sleep reflects a final fatality.
I gaze at his face, as frightened as mine, staring back at me.

2.

Goats nibble grass on a low hill,
bells tinkling far away.
The sun stops dead still
in heaven as if to say,
sadly, "A snake's toxins
poisoned her." Swallows
mourn her passing, but Death grins
as her boyfriend follows
her to the gaping hole she's left open
for his descent, a poet crying,
though heartbroken,
because of the mad women
who some day will behead him for his fantasy,
or call it his folly,
of believing his poems could save
anyone from dying.
Maybe to crave
immortality
is admirable, but poor Eurydice's

having to die
twice over is cruelty,
poetic
perhaps, but Hades is an empty,
barren place–
sunless, silent, deaf as a stone frieze–
where music
is useless and to look back is to see,
oh poet, as in a mirror, your vanity.

The Bassarids

1.

The enticing magic of ivy, fox, panther, pard,
of frenzied women, imbibed wine, an earthquake:
fast as it happens you make me discard
reason as if it were mere folly, a fake
Ionian law no one should obey lest the imprisoned
become the one who imprisons. I take
nothing back. I admit you'd cautioned
me you wouldn't stay, you the boy god
with the golden locks I couldn't keep
away from. It was at night along the esplanade
as we walked hand in hand–never to sleep
alone again, I boasted–that I first heard in the sea's
waves crashing on the beach how nothing safe frees
us from passion, a dark once seen inside us too deep
to deny. Like our ecstatic cries for our joined lawless bodies.

2.

I dream of us in the eastern Mediterranean
on an island, Samos, say, lapping waves,
fellow sailors, grape vines, olive trees, you a tan,
tall man standing on the beach by caves
an archaeologist is exploring, the cliffs' faces
basalt, sandstone, marble. There are many traces
of ancient ways in this strange place, flutes,
crotales, drums in the air, men round a fosse
passing wine bowls, singing. New shoots
of oregano, siderite, and sage. This is what loss
of you means to me, though I don't know why.
A wild dog howls by one of the moss-
covered pits. Maybe it is hungry. It is night. If I try
to find you near me as I sleep I will look where the sea
soars to greet you, your eyes a green brighter than dew on ivy.

3.

And the calm of our ensuing mornings, not a fantasy
exactly but a truth more like it, like a man
standing dockside waiting for a boat to carry
him somewhere unknown, without a plan
for his voyage to an unnamed island,
unmapped, strange, remote,
near stark mountains, plane trees, gold sand,
grape must, grottos, high cliffs, a goat
or two nipping at fennel, gentle oars
plashing in shallows. How easily I fall asleep
imagining, as I drift off, you are coming back
to me, all our windows and doors
open wide to welcome you, swallows flying, swallows
nesting in our bedroom as noon follows
noon with a light so glaring that, fiery as yours, it casts no shadows.

4.

The long sea journey we embark on like a night flight
of birds, guided by stars over deserts,
vast pinnacles, empty spaces. Requite
my love, my love. My heart hurts
without you. Creeks run dry. White-
washed houses, cold hearths, a thousand
bare rooms in an alien land.
I search in each one only to find you not
beside me but apart in the silence
where you wait on a rocky shore listening to the plaint
of women's voices coming closer. It is a hot
night. I'm sweating. It's been years since
I last saw you. Bees hover near the herb garden
you planted. Honey in the hive. What constraint
holds you back? Two lovers riven by a god's mad passion, now as then?

VI

D. 960

I wonder what music my friend Steve heard
in his head near the end. Schubert,
possibly, whom he loved. He'd said no word
is worth one note of his last sonata. It hurt
him to be leaving life. He worshipped all artful things
without reserve or hesitation. What does one say
to someone dying, wasting away from cancer?
On his last night alive, Jay called me. My phone rings
and rings until I answer it again. Yesterday
I saw a pigeon hit by a car, its broken wings
flapping on the street, desperate to fly free
of its death. The night my father fell asleep never
to awake, trees illuminated by heat lightning's
power blazed like a soul outside my window. Two fates sever
us from our precious lives. The silent god, and the one that sings.

The Mahler Sixth

A man might dream a meadow's dreams
of flowering. Or a girl's dreams as she
sleeps on sweet spring grass. A stream's
as it meanders, rambling, rippling softly,
through Bohemian woods. An old soldier's
as he snores by birch trees, his pipe
set aside, dreaming of love, the wars
he'd seen. A child's dreaming of a life
singing with angelic choirs. A plain stand
of ash dreaming of May's leaves and sap.
Or a man's restless dreaming of his homeland's
woods, wildernesses, awe-filled, map-
less places, frightening until one night,
as if he were no longer sleeping, moonlight
having brought him home to safety, its brass bands
in the village square play until all is once more right.

It's not easy, as mourners know, to dream as the world
dreams, to lie buried by earth's dreams,
needing to dig deeper, to be curled
in its belly, the bones each graveyard teems
with, cerecloth and tombs, wind sounds,
Alpine horns, cowbells in some faraway
summer, buglers in the valley, school grounds
with children shouting, laughing as day
nears its end. The sun-lit, soft brown mosses
the boy Mahler picked off stones along the trails
felt like tufts of his mother's hair. A symphony's
like that, too, like a man's dreaming of an Austrian
cemetery, cypress dimly seen before twilight fails
or the light sets from a dying child's eyes: all that began
when he first dreamed his lifelong dreams of oblivion
inextricable from his intensest joys, the music of his reveries.

Rothko Chapel

April is still wintery, the beach cool though
past dawn the mist hovering over
the ocean burns off. Like an early Rothko,
the sea's light looks born from water,
its surface taut as a stretched linen canvas.
Colors drift and shift, lift and fall, stirred
by undercurrents, chalk white, cloud gray, grass
green, feathery cobalt. The cliff walls, bruised
by tides, are a solemn, deep black: maroon-,
blue-tinted like the murals in the chapel. A glow
is emanating from the world's small things, pebbles,
shells, bits of glass, glittering ferns, leaves. By noon,
the sun shines blindingly, casting few shadows
to mute its intensity, the land starkly bright, the sea's
black somber gray like a mirror of last night's clouded moon.

Herz und Mund und Tat und Leben

> Art is born of humiliation.
> W.H. Auden

1.

A dead striped bass floats, alone,
in shallows. Kelp, driftwood,
a cracked jar, flat stone,
scattered shells, tangled seaweed:
washed-up things, neither good
nor sinister. What I need:
wave after wave of rhythms
to submit to, an immensity
to claim me, sea-surge hymns
at dawn relentlessly
pounding the shore. Anemones
flower in the pools by cliffside
caves, each a venomous blue. I've lied
my life through. Hurt whom I please.

2.

You walked me home, kissed me,
then left for the last time.
Now you're the one I see
when I tell my story, in rhyme
after rhyme, the beauty
I once knew, green eyes,
red hair, muscular body
that caught all by surprise
the moment you walked into
a room. Images of you I conjure
to save me from a death
I've long despised. Assure
me, love, that at my last breath
what I see will be as consoling as you.

3.

What remains when a life fails
for lack of its justification?
Clouds white as ships' sails
ride winds as if on a mission
to a people in need of rain.
What if I have believed
in all the wrong things,
nothing I've conceived
of real? White sand, empty
sky, white sun—morning's
arrived too clear to see by.
I wait for night, for darkness
to return, starless, blank, colorless
as the void that reigned before creation.

4.

The beach is deserted. Smoke bellows,
acrid, from a downwind fire.
The ocean is a glazed black gray,
flat as slate. Where the wind blows
loudest, it sounds like a choir,
harmonious and profound. Day
is curled in the arms of night,
like you in mine, one hope indistinguishable
from the other, the visible invisible
world of love and memory.
A coal black ship sails westward,
like a man headed toward
his death. Night looms over the sea,
obscuring the horizon, no end to its journey.

5.

Humiliation is like a gift sometimes,
a grace, a nakedness, the soul
prepared, stripped bare
for its unmaking. As the sun climbs
over hills, I stroll
the beach in search of shards, no care
for tomorrow. More bad stories
on the news, wars, disease,
great cities' ruination. Poems
might be our stay against abjection,
the art we concoct as if at a whim
of fate we've been denied the only homes
we've known: how I loved him
when life for a while felt moved by perfection.

In the Eagerness of Boyish Hope, after Wordsworth

In a Carolina old growth forest, what I'd seen was not fact
exactly, not a mystery otherwise revealed by noon's full
transparency but virgin pine or oak trees that had left a track,
a trace of what once flourished there, shadows that pull
a boy in deeper, the odor of dripping ferns, wet stones
in the air, the rustle of small creatures scurrying across
needle-, leaf-strewn ground where mouldering pelts and bones
lie buried and limbs and branches sparkle shrouded by moss.
History is loss. History is tribulation. Rubble and ash.
The sealed tomb. Lost in backwoods, in my lucky youth,
I stood naked in a cooling creek on water-worn sandstone
as a rushing cascade pounded on me like waves, breaking, crash-
ing onto my body while I exalted in what I believed to be a lasting truth:
the forceful shade cast by woods in late summer and a roaring fall's unknown
power would show me how like I was to immortality if I'd trace it back to its source.

Canticum Sacrum

The light of stars seems never to die. Recall the lamps lit
by wise virgins who'd saved
enough oil for the bridegroom
who came after nightfall
while the wicks still flamed. Sit
by the sea. Listen to his music being played
on the radio behind you in the evening gloom.
Imagine Byzantine domes, mosaic and gold, by a lapping canal

as the chorus' voices transport his body
on a flower-draped gondola
over lagoons, by the sea
to San Michele,
as close to La Serenissima
as he is to God, where he lies under cypress' funereal beauty.

Dawn's mist rises off a muted Lido.
Ships' flags
flap on a breezy
morning as a red-throated loon zigzags
over the piazza, San Marco,
Venice crowned
in glory
by the sun at its zenith like the carved marble sound

of his music, its vaulting naves, domes, bell towers,
or, in Cannaregio,
the lions' mouths spouting spring-clear waters

into the basins below
while in the silent canticle
of its plain flat stone you contemplate the grave of Igor Stravinsky.

Peter Weltner was raised in northern New Jersey and piedmont North Carolina. He graduated from Hamilton College (A.B.) and Indiana University (Ph.D.). For thirty seven years, he taught American, British, and Irish literature at San Francisco State University.

He has published twenty five books or chapbooks of fiction and poetry, and his work over the years has appeared in numerous literary magazines and journals. He was awarded two O. Henrys for his short stories. His most recent titles are *In the Half Light* (Brick House Books), *Bird and Tree/In Place*, and *Scrapbooks Mappings of My Country* (both Marrowstone Press). He lives with his husband of thirty five years, Atticus Carr, in San Francisco, steps away from the Pacific.

www.ingramcontent.com/pod-product-compliance
Lightning Source LLC
Chambersburg PA
CBHW022019290426
44109CB00015B/1241